MW00699761

Late Elementary through Interm

SUCCEEDING WITH THE MASTERS®

BAROQUE ERA, Volume One

Compiled and edited by Helen Marlais

About the Series

Succeeding with the Masters® is a series dedicated to the authentic keyboard works of the Baroque, Classical, Romantic, and Twentieth-Century masters.

This series provides a complete and easily accessible method for learning and performing the works of the masters. Each book presents the works in historical perspective for the student, and provides the means and the motivation to play these pieces in the correct stylistic, musical, and technical manner. The easily understandable format of practice strategies and musical concepts make this series enjoyable for both students and teachers.

To ensure authenticity, all of these pieces have been extensively researched. Teachers will find a wealth of excellent repertoire that can be used for recitals, festivals, competitions, and state achievement testing. Many of these original compositions may be new to you while others will be familiar. This series brings together an essential and comprehensive library of the pedagogical repertoire of the great composers.

Succeeding with the Masters® begins with late-elementary repertoire, continues through intermediate-level works and also includes a few early-advanced works. Upon completion of this series, students will be well prepared for the entry-level sonatas by the master composers.

THE
F·J·H
MUSIC
COMPANY
INC.
Frank J. Hackinson

Production: Frank and Gail Hackinson
Production Coordinators: Philip Groeber and Isabel Otero Bowen
Cover: Terpstra Design, San Francisco - in collaboration with Helen Marlais
Cover: Chalk lithograph of J. S. Bach from the *Pougin Iconography Collection*, Sibley Music Library
Text Design and Layout: Susan Pinkerton
Engraving: Tempo Music Press, Inc.
Printer: Tempo Music Press, Inc.

ISBN-13: 978-1-56939-448-9

PREFACE

A Note for Teachers and Students

Succeeding with the Masters®, Baroque Era Volume One, is a collection of graded repertoire featuring the great masters of the Baroque era. These works, mostly dances, build a foundation for playing more advanced baroque music. Each piece is introduced with a short "discovery" of a particular characteristic of the Baroque era. Brief segments on "practice strategies" guide the student in how to prepare and perform the piece. This comprehensive approach to learning style, technique, and historical context provides a valuable foundation for successful performance of all baroque repertoire pieces.

Two icons are used throughout the volume:

Characteristics of the Baroque Era

indicates the Musical Characteristics of the Baroque era

Practice Strategy

outlines a practice strategy or illustrates a musical concept that guides the student in how to learn more efficiently and play more musically.

Many published collections take great liberties in altering pitches, rhythms, and articulations that the composers clearly did not intend. The pieces in this collection, however, are based on facsimiles of the composer's own manuscripts, and on Urtext editions, which are editions that reflect the composer's original intent. From these scores, the editor has created performance scores for the student.

- Since these composers did not supply dynamic marking or fingerings, all of the dynamics and fingerings are editorial and are intended as a guide for students as they explore the baroque style.
- These composers supplied very few articulation and phrase markings, so many of these markings are also editorial.
- Editorial metronome markings are added as a guide.
- Ornaments have been realized for the student and appear as ossias above or below the staff.
- The downloadable recordings include complete performances and a practice strategy workshop. For a complete list of track numbers, see page six. To learn how to download the free recordings and use them as a valuable practice aid, turn to the inside back cover.

MUSIC DURING THE BAROQUE ERA (1600–1750)

During this era composers started writing specifically for one instrument, as compared to writing pieces for singers or for a group of musicians. Baroque composers of keyboard music supplied titles that related to dance movements and to popular titles of the day, such as Minuet, Gavotte, Toccata, Prelude, Aria, and Theme and Variations. The minuet became the most popular dance form of all, and its importance can be seen by how many minuets were written. In Bach's day, the minuet was quite lively, but later, in the Classical era, the minuets became more dignified and slower. Keyboard pieces were often comprised of successive dance movements, usually arranged in "Suites." These movements were the Allemande, Courante, Sarabande, and Gigue, and they were often interspersed with other dances.

MUSICAL CHARACTERISTICS OF THE BAROQUE ERA:

- Rhythm is one of the most distinctive elements, with a steady beat and regular accents.
- Pieces often have a compelling energy that endures until the end.
- Many pieces have a perpetual motion.
- Melodies are usually made up of short phrase fragments of irregular lengths.
- Works use recurring rhythmic or melodic patterns.
- Small details are repeated, changed slightly, and not just duplicated.
- Imitation is used.
- Phrases are not symmetrical.
- Polyphonic texture is prevalent, meaning a melodic line in one hand is usually combined with an equally important line in the other hand.
- There might be two melodic lines within the same hand, each called a "voice."
- Ornamentation is used (trills, mordents, *appoggiaturas*, turns).
- Sections of pieces often end with an ornament that resolves to the last note.
- Usually one mood is expressed in a baroque piece (if a piece begins happily, it ends happily).
- Binary and ternary forms are used.

Saint Nicholas Church, Prague.

This baroque church, designed by Kilian Ignaz Dientzenhofer, was completed in 1735. The very decorative nature of baroque buildings provides a visual example of the style of the time.

What the student will learn in Volume One:

Characteristics of the era:

J.S. Bach pieces:

Handel pieces:

Scarlatti pieces:

Helen Marlais's Practice Strategies®:

Volume One – Late Elementary through Intermediate Repertoire

The pieces within each composer category are arranged in order of difficulty, with the least difficult pieces immediately following the short biography of the composer.

For a complete list of sources for these pieces, see page 82.

Download all tracks for free! See inside back cover for information.

FOR THE STUDENT —
BAROQUE PERFORMANCE PRACTICE

To play baroque music beautifully, remember that most baroque keyboard pieces are fundamentally dances.

The feeling of two, three, four, or even one beat to the bar must permeate your whole body and mind. When you play these pieces, the rhythm of the music must carry you and make you feel like dancing.

Performers during the Baroque era were accustomed to following a set of rules, or musical conventions, which were appropriate and tasteful. These rules were applied to four basic musical points — tempo, dynamics, articulation, and ornamentation.

Tempo
Choosing an appropriate tempo helps to set the overall mood of the piece. Rhythm is perhaps the most distinctive element of baroque music, so keeping a steady beat with regular accents is extremely important.

Dynamics
Composers rarely wrote dynamic markings in their works for two reasons: The instruments of the day did not have a large dynamic range, and they trusted the performer to know the style and play accordingly. Therefore, it is up to the performer playing on a modern-day instrument, to add dynamics that show contrast within a work, that balance the character or mood of the piece, and that are stylistically appropriate. C.P. E. Bach, one of J.S. Bach's sons, wrote in his *Essay on the True Art of Playing Keyboard Instruments*, that it was customary to play complete passages or sections *forte* the first time, *piano* the second. To see what kinds of instruments the pieces in this book were actually played on, turn to page 20.

Articulation
Refers to how notes are attacked, accented, sustained, and phrased. In baroque keyboard literature, each note must be articulated with the best possible clarity. Phrasing refers to the separation of notes into single notes or notes in pairs or groups. Composers rarely wrote articulation or phrase markings in their works because the performance practice of the day was generally understood. For example, during the Baroque era, performers would lift their hand after short slurs in order to hear a break between shorter note values and longer note values, and especially before downbeats. Since they could not create dynamic change, breaks in sound would create accent and give the illusion of dynamics.

Today, we can use more dynamics and a greater range of articulations, so our style can be different but appropriate for the same music. A simple rule to follow for adapting these pieces to the piano, however, is the following: quarter notes are to be played *non legato*, while eighth notes are to be played *legato*; or if the piece is made up of eighth and sixteenth notes, then the sixteenth notes are played *legato* while the eighth notes are played *non legato*.

Melodic motives are often *legato*, whereas wide intervals are *non legato*. It is important that both the attack and the release of the note be well emphasized. Fingering is of paramount importance because of the complexity of the moving lines. Learn the correct fingering from the very beginning, and use the same fingering all of the time.

Two examples from Bach's music:

Excerpt from "Minuet in C minor"

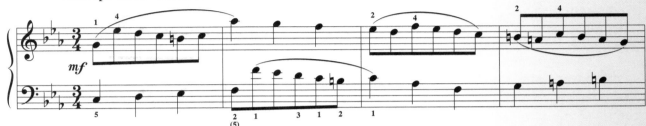

Excerpt from "Musette in D major"

At times, notes with the same duration are not always played equally. In Handel's music, for example, successive quarter notes can be played as follows, with the first beat of the slur sounding stronger than the second beat:

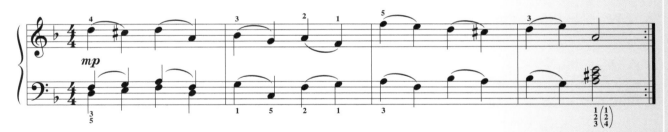

Excerpt from "Aria"

Ornamentation

Ornamentation was the way baroque composers "filled out" the texture and made the sound more elaborate and grand. Even when ornaments were not written in, it was customary for the performer to add them, improvised! It was especially customary to add embellishments on the repeats of sections and at the ends of sections. The most common ornaments are:

The trill: ✦✦ or 𝄊𝄊   The trill is always played on the beat, starting on the *upper* note.

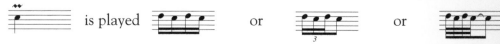

Your choice of how to execute the trill will depend on the musical context.

The mordent: ✸

The mordent adds brilliance to notes and is always played on the beat, starting on the main note. This three-note embellishment begins on the *principal* note, goes down, and then back up. Mordents are often used in ascending melodic lines.

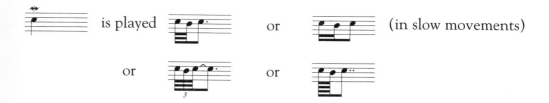

The turn: ∾

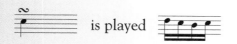

The turn is added to make the music more expressive, one of the chief aims of composers during the Baroque era. The turn consists of four notes that start on the beat. Beginning on the *upper* note, the main note is played, then the note below, and back up to the main note. The turn is always played as a musical extension of the melodic line.

The *appoggiatura*: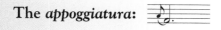

The *appoggiatura* is played on the beat and receives half of the duration of the principal note. The accent is on the *appoggiatura* and not on the principal note. This ornament should be played expressively.

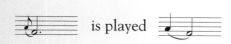

Use of the pedal
The instruments of the era did not have a pedal, so the music in this volume does not use pedal markings. Pedal can be used in some cases, however, for a slight sustaining effect.

JOHANN SEBASTIAN BACH

(1685–1750)

J.S. Bach was born in Eisenach, Germany, in the central part of the country. He came from a family of musicians, and as a boy he sang and studied the harpsichord, violin, clavichord, and organ. His father was his first music teacher. Johann Sebastian lost both his parents when he was a young boy. His mother passed away when he was only nine. When his father passed away just before he turned ten, his older brother Johann Christoph became his guardian and teacher.

When Bach was fifteen, he went to sing in the choir of St. Michael's Church in Lüneburg, where he received a general education as well as a musical one. Since he had to earn his own money, he also played in the church orchestra. At an early age, Bach was known to study and work a great deal, and he had a large appetite for acquiring knowledge.

Bach was a master keyboard player. Over the course of his lifetime, he held many positions in the Lutheran Church in various German cities, as an organist and a music director. He was so busy with his posts and he composed so much music that he never had time to travel outside of Germany!

Bach was very well known as an organist and teacher, but it was long after his death before people began to realize how amazing his compositions were. His primary instrument was the organ. Although the pianoforte was created during his lifetime (around 1709), he only played one a few times, and he hardly ever composed any music for it. He played the harpsichord and the clavichord, and the music he wrote for those instruments is performed primarily on the piano today.

Bach was married twice, and had 20 children — eleven sons and nine daughters. Only ten children survived infancy. His second wife, Anna Magdalena, taught their children keyboard lessons, and Johann Sebastian compiled two notebooks for her, filled with teaching pieces. The first notebook was presented to her in Cöthen in 1722, and the second in Leipzig in 1725. Imagine someone special giving you a beautiful compilation of pieces, complete with an elaborate cover with edges gilded in gold! Some of the pieces were Bach's own compositions, while others were composed by his son Carl Philipp Emanuel. Some were written by friends of the Bach family, and, as you will see in this volume, no one knows to this day who wrote some of them.

A man named Wolfgang Schmieder researched and organized all of Bach's works and the abbreviation BWV stands for *Bach Werke Verzeichnis*, or Bach Works Catalogue. When you see the abbreviation "Anh" after the BWV number, it means the work can be found in the Catalogue Appendix ("Anhang" means Appendix).

*Portrait of J. S. Bach by Johann Jakob Ihle - *Sammlung Bachhaus Eisenach/Neue Bachgesellschaft e.V.*

Theme in F major

The original title of this piece is "Satz," the German word for a movement, or a theme. We do not know who wrote this piece, but J.S. Bach placed it in a notebook of pieces he dedicated to his wife, Anna Magdalena. You can read about this notebook in the biography of J.S. Bach on page 10.

In baroque music, melodies are usually made up of short phrases of irregular, differing lengths. In the A section below, the two brackets show that the first phrase is three measures long, while the second phrase is four measures long!

Characteristics of the Baroque Era

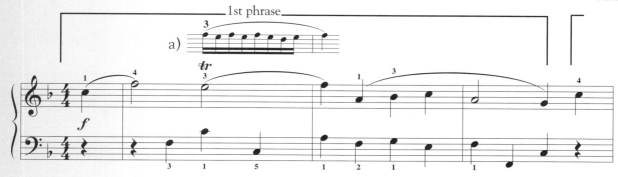

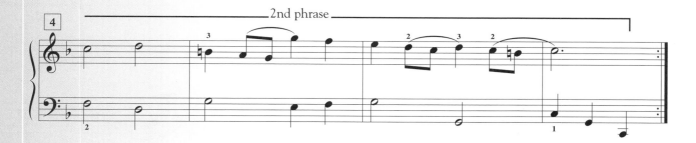

Shaping phrases:

Practice the three circled phrase fragments shown below, listening to the natural *crescendo* to the longest and highest note of the phrase. Remember that shorter note values, such as eighth notes, want to lead to long note values, such as quarter and half notes, without any breaks in between.

Practice Strategy

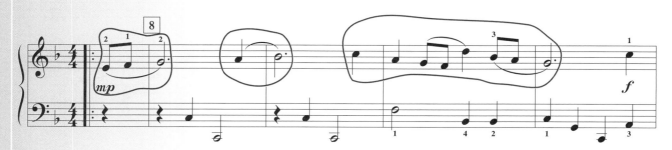

THEME IN F MAJOR

Composer unknown
BWV Anh. 131

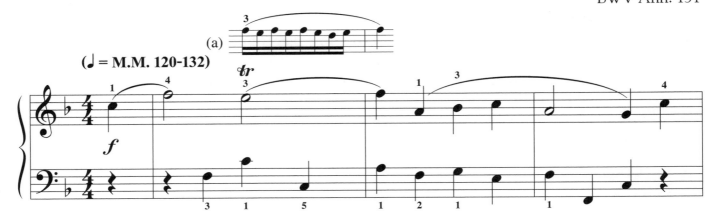

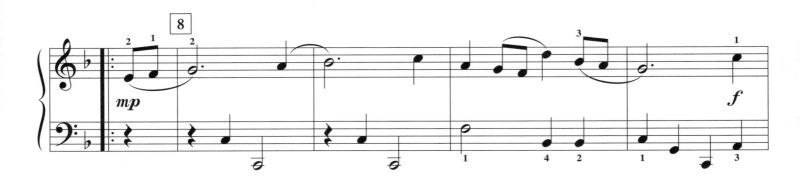

(a) This piece may be played without the trill, or can be played as:

MINUET IN G MAJOR

This piece was written by a friend of the Bach family, Christian Pezold, who lived from 1677–1733. An organist and composer, Pezold spent the bulk of his career in Dresden; he was appointed court organist by 1697, and court chamber composer in 1709. One of Europe's most famous organists of the early eighteenth century, he made concert tours to such locations as Paris (1714) and Venice (1716). Very few of his compositions survive, but this famous one is found in the *Anna Magdalena Bach Notebook.*

Observe in this Minuet:

- Use of binary form (AB)
- Use of one recurring rhythmic pattern. Clap and count the following pattern four times in a row so that it will be natural to you.

Characteristics of the Baroque Era

Adding ornamentation:

Baroque composers used ornamentation to "fill out" the texture and sustain the sound through long notes. The overall sound, then, was more elaborate and grand. Even when ornaments were not written in, it was customary for the performer to add them, improvised! Ornaments should always be played musically as an extension of the melodic line. Only after you have learned this Minuet well *without* the ornaments will it be time to add them.

Practice Strategy

In the box below, observe the ending of the Minuet. Experiment with playing a trill, a mordent, and then a turn. Decide for yourself which one you would like to play in this measure to end the piece!

Measure 31–end:

Refer to pages eight and nine for more ideas on how to ornament piece.

MINUET IN G MAJOR

Christian Pezold
BWV Anh. 114

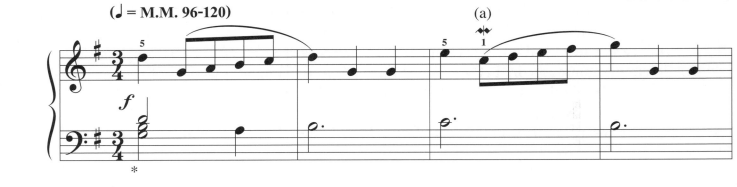

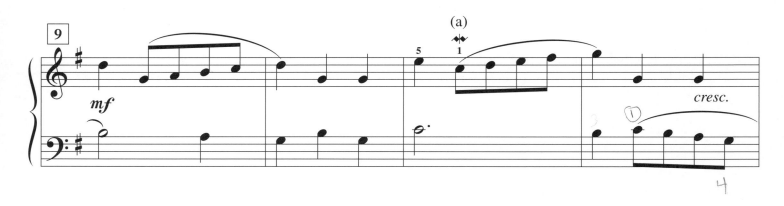

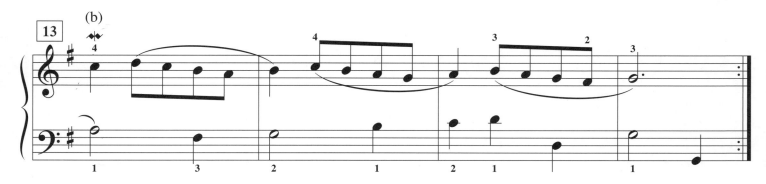

*N.B. Quarter notes should be played slightly detached, unless marked otherwise.

The first note of the mordent begins *on* the beat.

FJH1438

(d) Optional trill:

FJH1438

MUSETTE IN D MAJOR

In the seventeenth and early part of the eighteenth century in France, the "musette" was a small bagpipe that the aristocracy used. Because of the repetitive figure in the left hand, this particular piece might suggest the drone of a bagpipe. No one knows who wrote this lively piece that Bach chose to include in the notebook he dedicated to his wife, Anna Magdalena, in 1725.

Characteristics of the Baroque Era

Characteristics of the Baroque era exemplified in this piece:

- Use of an ostinato bass
  Note in the full score the bass line that is repeated over and over again.

Characteristics of the Baroque Era

- Usually only one mood is expressed in a baroque piece, as compared to the Classical era, when a "contrast of mood" during a piece was very important. Musettes have a pastoral character, which means that you can think of a country scene when you are playing the piece. Below are some adjectives that might describe the single mood of this musette. Circle one adjective you think best characterizes this piece.

heroic	*mournful*	*impressive*
bright	*fearless*	*cheerful*
joyful	*nervous*	*edgy*

Practice Strategy

"Play-Prepare":

This strategy assists with learning the notes and fingerings of a piece with great accuracy and precision.

Step One: Play from the beginning of the piece to the end of measure two. Then stop. Look ahead! Move your hands quickly and silently to *prepare* your fingers over the next downbeat, circled below.

Step Two: Check to see that your fingers are on the correct keys, and then *play* the notes.

Step Three: Now practice the "play-prepare" strategy from measures three to five, and from measures seven to nine. Practicing this repeatedly will ensure that you always play the correct keys with the correct fingering!

Practicing the first measure:

1) Play with a slight accent on every downbeat. Let your wrist drop and relax on the first note. (See example below.)

2) Once you have made a beautiful, warm sound, lift your wrist while rolling up on your finger until you are playing the key with the fleshy part of your finger. Remember to roll your finger and wrist towards the fallboard of the piano.

A technical motion essential for playing the three-note and four-note slurs is shown below. Practice this gesture until it feels secure and comfortable.

The left-hand accompaniment must be playful and steady, always providing a supportive framework for the right-hand melody. The rhythm must have a lively, pulsating quality. As you practice this piece, listen for each and every note to be well articulated. If you lose clarity, you are playing the piece too quickly.

MUSETTE IN D MAJOR

Composer unknown
BWV Anh. 126

*Another
articulation
idea:

KEYBOARD INSTRUMENTS OF THE BAROQUE ERA

The most important keyboard instruments of the Baroque era were the harpsichord, the clavichord, and the organ. All of the pieces in this book were composed for either the harpsichord or the clavichord.

The harpsichord is different from the piano in many ways. The most significant difference is that the strings are plucked, not struck. The earliest reference to a harpsichord is from the year 1397, in Italy. Harpsichords are still performed on today.

Two-Manual Harpsichord made by
Johannes Couchet, *circa* 1650

*courtesy of The Metropolitan Museum of Art, The Crosby Brown
Collection of Musical Instruments, 1889 (89.4.2363) Photograph,
all rights reserved, The Metropolitan Museum of Art.*

The clavichord was used from the fifteenth century to the nineteenth century. It was commonly used to practice, learn, and compose on. Sound is produced when a small brass blade strikes the string. The sound is controlled by the performer, and it is very, very quiet, from *ppp* to *mp*! Today, there are still people around the world who are passionate about playing the clavichord.

Unfretted Clavichord, late 17th or 18th century

*courtesy of The Metropolitan Museum of Art,
The Crosby Brown Collection of Musical Instruments, 1889 (89.4.1207)
Photograph, all rights reserved, The Metropolitan Museum of Art.*

MINUET IN G MINOR

This piece was written before the year 1707, when Bach visited
the German town of Lübeck, which was inspiring to him
because of the many evening concerts.

Use of the popular minuet:

The minuet is a dance of French origin, usually in triple meter, to be played at a moderate to brisk tempo. The minuet evolved in tempo and style from the Baroque through Classical eras but remained popular with the upper class until the late eighteenth century.

**Characteristics
of the
Baroque Era**

Many baroque pieces follow either a binary or rounded binary form.

Binary

**(two parts, different
melodic material in each section)**

Rounded Binary

**(when part of the A section returns in
the B section)**

**Characteristics
of the
Baroque Era**

Looking at the full score, this Minuet has what form? Mark with a star ★ the A section, mark with an X the B section, and if you see the A section return in your score, mark it with a star ★ .

Practicing with the metronome:

This technique not only helps you to play evenly and steadily, but it also helps you to give each note its full durational value, which is extremely important in playing baroque music. Since each note must be articulated with the best possible clarity and focus, consistent practice with the metronome will guide you in becoming a good player!

**Practice
Strategy**

Always remember that rhythm is a distinctive element of the Baroque era, and keeping a steady beat with regular accents is very important.

Set the metronome at ♩ = M.M. 60. Practice hands separately at first, then hands together. When you are comfortable with this speed, you can increase it. Once you can do this easily, set the metronome at 60 to the ♩., feeling one beat per bar. This will help to create a dance-like minuet feel.

Remember, the metronome helps you develop an inner pulse!

Minuet in G minor

Johann Sebastian Bach
BWV 822

MINUET IN D MINOR

This piece, by an unknown composer, was chosen by Bach for the notebook he dedicated to his wife, Anna Magdalena, in 1725. To learn more about this famous notebook, you can read J.S. Bach's biography on page 10.

Characteristics of the Baroque Era

An extremely important characteristic of the Baroque era, polyphonic texture, is found in this piece. This means that a melodic line in the right hand is combined with an equally important bass line.

Practice Strategy

Creating clear sixteenth-note patterns:

The following two sixteenth-note rhythmic patterns are found in this piece.

With the metronome set at ♪ = M.M. 88, count out loud while tapping the following rhythms. Continue to count and tap each line without stopping so you feel the forward direction of the rhythm.

Continue each line without stopping!

After you can do this easily, isolate the measures in your score and circle (with a pencil!) all of the sixteenth-note patterns. Playing each measure correctly four times in a row will help you to play this piece with ease and confidence!

Shaping the left-hand phrases:

When playing polyphonic music, it is important to bring out both melodic lines of music. In the next example you see the first three phrases of the Minuet. The left-hand phrases have been numbered for you. In each phrase, slightly *crescendo* to the highest note, and then taper (*decrescendo*) to the end of the phrase.

Practice Strategy

Be sure to shape all of the left-hand phrases of the piece so that both melodic lines are interesting to listen to, and both help give the feeling of dance.

Minuet in D minor

Composer unknown
BWV Anh. 132

(a) This ornament, called a *schleifer*, or "slide," is played as indicated above the measure.
The slide begins *on* the beat.

MINUET IN G MAJOR

Characteristics of the Baroque Era

Rhythm is one of the most distinctive elements of baroque dance music, with its steady beat and regular accents. Listen to the recording of this piece and tap the rhythm of the piece. Notice that the triple meter is always steady and energetic.

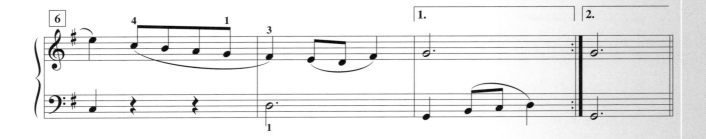

Practice Strategy

Activating rhythmic patterns:

In order to convey the dance spirit of this and other baroque pieces, it is important to "energize" your fingers and make every note articulated and vibrant, as if your fingers are excited and doing something they love!

When you see a five-note slur that starts in one measure and goes *through* the bar line, *lead* (without rushing!) to the downbeat, or "activate" every note of the short phrase segment, like this:

"Energize" your fingers!

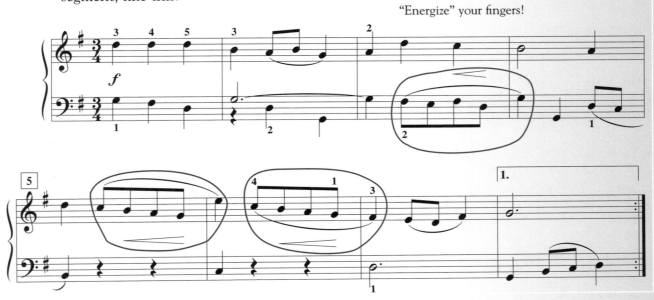

When you see three quarter notes in a measure, you may gently *crescendo through* the measure and over the bar line, to help you lead through the passage:

How to play a measure written for a large hand:

Practice Strategy

If you have a small hand, you will notice that the left-hand part in measure 12 cannot be played as Bach wrote it, with the dotted half note held for the duration of the measure.

In order to play this measure, you may change the note value of the first note so that you have time to move your hand to the A on the third beat:

This very small change from 𝅗𝅥. to 𝅗𝅥 𝄽 will help you to play this piece!

Minuet in G major

Johann Sebastian Bach
BWV 822

*N.B. The G in the bass may be played again.

*N.B. Listen to the recording to hear the subtle change in phrasing on the repeat from measures 13-15 and 21-end.

Bach's childhood home in Eisenach, Germany.
Bachhaus in Eisenach - *Sammlung Bachhaus Eisenach/Neue Bachgesellschaft e.V.*

MINUET IN G

Although this is one of the most famous pieces for the keyboard, we do not know who wrote it! Obviously, Bach thought it was a good piece, since he chose it for his own children's musical education, and placed it in the *Anna Magdalena Bach Notebook.* Students still play this piece almost 300 years later!

Characteristics of the Baroque Era

Taking a look at the Minuet on pages 33 and 34, notice that it is in $\frac{3}{4}$ time, and there is a theme that is presented in one hand and then soon after in the other hand. This is called "imitation," because one hand copies, or imitates, the other!

Practice Strategy

How to shape phrases:

Look below at part of the Urtext* score of the opening of the *Minuet in G.* Notice that there are not any slurs placed over the notes.

Now look at part of the score that you will be learning. Each phrase can continue through the bar line, ending the musical idea, or motive, on the next downbeat.

*See Preface for the definition of "Urtext."

Minuet in G

Composer unknown
BWV Anh. 116

*N.B. All quarter notes may be played *non legato* or detached, depending on the performer's taste.

FJH1438

34

MINUET IN C MINOR

J.S. Bach wrote this *Minuet in C minor* and placed it in a
notebook he presented to his wife in 1722.

**Characteristics
of the
Baroque Era**

Pieces have perpetual motion.

During the Baroque era, pieces often seem to have few resting places. The forward
motion is characteristically felt from the beginning to the end.

**Practice
Strategy**

Take a look at the following section of the Minuet. The right hand can play a continuous
eighth-note phrase from measure 17 to measure 25! Practice this right-hand part,
focusing on the continuity of the musical line.

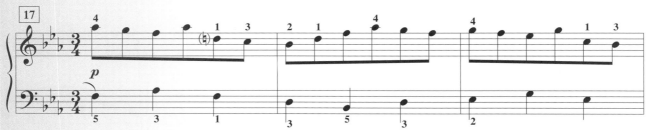

"8 times to perfection."

Practice sections in segments of one measure plus one downbeat at two different speeds
— one slow, the other, *a tempo*. In order to learn pieces as well as you possibly can, make
sure that you concentrate on playing the small segment with one hundred percent
accuracy and that you play the segment eight times *correctly*. Remember, practicing
begins when you play the segment *correctly*.

**Practice
Strategy**

MINUET IN C MINOR

Johann Sebastian Bach
BWV 813

(a) An optional trill may be played here.

*N.B. You can continue to play eighth-note phrases *legato*, in both the right and left hands.
C.P.E. Bach, one of J.S. Bach's sons, wrote in his *Essay on the True Art of Playing Keyboard Instruments*, that, "It was a convenient custom to indicate by appropriate marks only the first few of prolonged successions of *legato* or detached notes, it being self-evident that all of the tones are to be played similarly."

PRELUDE IN C MAJOR

This piece is part of a set of preludes composed and compiled by J.S. Bach, named *Five Little Preludes*.

Characteristics of the Baroque Era

Characteristics of the era exemplified in this piece:

- A piece from the Baroque era will often have an enduring energy. From the very beginning of the piece, there is motion and activity that does not stop until the final measure. This kind of action is exciting to the ear because the forward motion is great.

- Use of ornamentation: mordents in measures 9–11, and a trill in measure 15.

Practice Strategy

"Impulse" practicing:

There is only one measure in this entire piece that displays sixteenth notes. In order to play these cleanly, and so that they sparkle with excitement without rushing, separate this entire measure into four segments, or "impulses."

Measure 14:

Beats one to two:

Beats one to three:

Beats one to four:

Entire measure plus the next downbeat:

Practice with the metronome at the following speeds: ♩ = M.M. 72, and then ♩ = M.M. 100. Listen for absolute clarity and evenness. You can stop in the *middle* of each beat to further ensure that the notes are extremely clear and even.

PRELUDE IN C MAJOR

Johann Sebastian Bach
BWV 939

GEORGE FRIDERIC HANDEL

(1685–1759)

Handel was born in Halle, Germany, sixty miles from where J.S. Bach was born in the same year, although the two never met. He was baptized Georg Friederich Händel. Unlike other famous composers, Handel did not come from a musical family.

George showed signs of great musical interest when he was very young. His father wanted him to grow up to be a lawyer, and forbade an instrument in their home. But George loved music so much that he smuggled a small clavichord into the attic and practiced secretly! Handel's father begrudgingly let the boy take lessons on the organ, harpsichord, violin, and oboe, only after a reigning duke told him that his son had talent. By the early age of ten, Handel had given many performances and had written quite a bit of music.

In 1702, when George was seventeen years old, he began his studies at the University of Halle for law. His musical skill was such that at the age of eighteen he was appointed organist at the Calvinist Cathedral. After university studies, George moved to Hamburg, Germany. In those days operas were presented for the most part only in the courts of kings and queens, but Hamburg had a regular opera company, and Handel was inspired to write many of them.

In Hamburg, Handel made the acquaintance of Johann Mattheson, a man well versed in opera theater as a composer, keyboard player, and singer. One night, during a performance, the two quarreled, and the argument became so strong that they went outside, drew their swords, and fought. The story goes that Handel would have been killed, except that the sword broke against one of his metal coat buttons! After that close brush with death, the two made peace and became friends.

In 1706, at the age twenty-one, Handel moved to Italy. He lived in a palace in Rome, as an employee of the Marquis Francesco Ruspoli. In 1708, Ruspoli created a lavish set in the theater in his palace, for the production of Handel's first Italian opera. In the performance, there were forty-five orchestra members, a large number for the day. The audience, too, was large, and 1500 copies of the libretto (the operatic text) were printed for their use. In 1710, Handel left Italy a polished artist. Though his fame and notoriety continued to flourish, he always found time to teach private keyboard lessons. Many of the pieces you are playing in this volume are pieces that were taught to students by the great master himself!

*Chalk lithograph of G. F. Handel from the *Pougin Iconography Collection*, Sibley Music Library

MINUET IN G MAJOR

This minuet is from *Partita in G. Partita* is another word for "suite."

**Characteristics
of the
Baroque Era**

Keyboard pieces during the Baroque era were comprised mostly of dance-inspired movements, usually arranged in "suites," and the fundamental pieces were the Allemande, Courante, Sarabande, and Gigue. Often other dance movements were added, such as the Prelude, Minuet, and Air. All of the movements within a suite, or partita, are in the same key, but are different in tempo, meter, and character.

This piece is in binary form.

Binary form means that a piece is comprised of two parts. The A section has different melodic material than the B section, and the sections are set apart from each other with repeat signs. In this piece, both sections end on the tonic (G major). Label these two parts, A and B, in your full score.

**Characteristics
of the
Baroque Era**

How to create a dance feel:

Once you are technically secure with this piece, it is time to think about how to create a feeling of the baroque dance, in order to bring this piece to life musically.

Here are three ways to succeed:

1) With the metronome, practice feeling one beat per bar. It is important to feel the dance rhythm go through your body and out through your fingers with each phrase.

2) Decide where the phrase goals are. The phrase goals are the places toward which the music naturally moves. Let your ear be your guide and listen to this rise of melody toward the goal. After this goal, the phrase naturally tapers. The A section has been marked for you below.

3) Sometimes, imagining that both parts of the music could be played by instruments of the baroque orchestra helps to make the sound more real. For instance, the left-hand part could be a stringed instrument, and the right-hand part could be a recorder or a flute. Dance or walk around the room in tempo while you listen to the recording so that you feel the piece as a dance!

**Practice
Strategy**

Minuet in G major

George Frideric Handel
from *Partita in G*

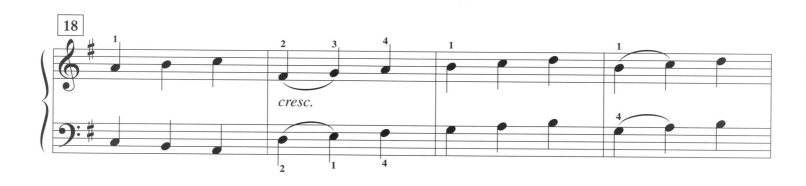

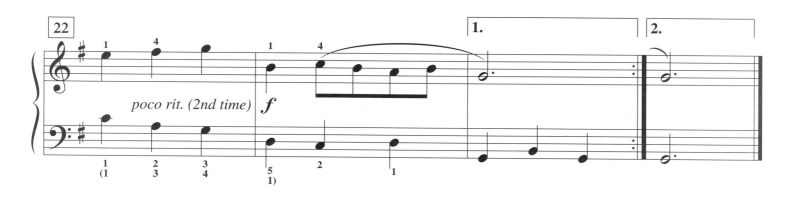

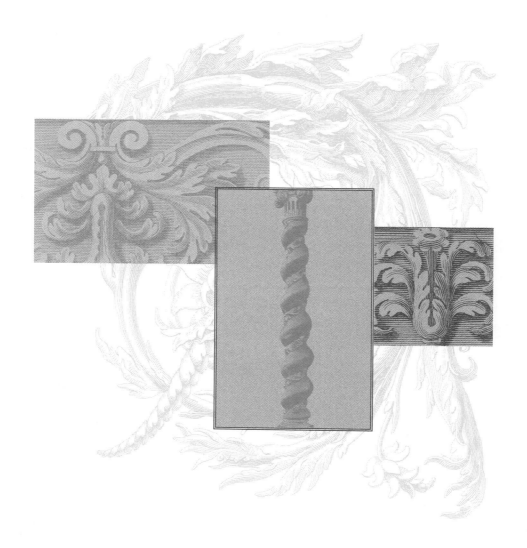

IMPERTINENCE

This piece has an interesting title. When you listen to the recording,
look up the definition of the word in a dictionary.

**Characteristics
of the
Baroque Era**

Characteristics of the era observed in this piece:
- Recurring rhythmic and melodic patterns
- Both sections of the piece end with an ornament that resolves to the last note.
- Use of a countermelody

Understanding countermelodies:
Sometimes an important melody is accompanied by a new melody, called a
countermelody. Do you notice, in the example below, that the melody in the right hand
begins, and then the left-hand melody begins before the right hand has finished? The
same occurs in measures three and four. The countermelodies in the left hand are being
very insistent, as if it is a conversation. The left hand is even being a bit stubborn,
coming in before the right hand has finished!

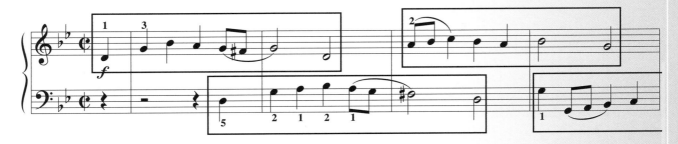

**Practice
Strategy**

How to play baroque articulations:
Since the keyboard instruments of the era were very different from the modern-day
piano, performers had different concerns that we must carefully consider.

Experiment in the following ways:
Lightly accent every quarter note in the piece that is followed by eighth notes. To
accent, play in a semi-detached manner, with a fine and slight emphasis of the notes.
First, play the quarter notes semi-detached, and then play them all with a *staccato* touch.
Do you hear the difference in the articulation?

First play:

Then play:

Then, for every eighth-note pattern, try not to force the first note. Instead, a small
crescendo through the second eighth note all the way to the longest note of the short
phrase is best. This will help to give the piece energy and rhythmic drive.

Turn to page 20 to see what keyboard instruments you would have played, if you had
lived during the Baroque era!

Impertinence

George Frideric Handel
HWV 494

(a) Optional trills:

FJH1438

A step in the minuet - *The Art of Dancing*
by Kellom Tomlinson, 1735

MINUET IN F MAJOR

This minuet displays three characteristics of the era.

Characteristics of the Baroque Era

- Rhythm as the most distinctive element, with a steady beat and regular accents.
- Use of rounded binary form, which means that part of the A section returns in the B section. (Please see page 21 for a discussion on form.) Mark in the score where this A section returns.
- A trill announces cadences at the ends of sections.

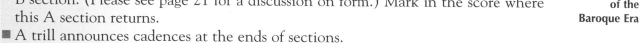

How to create a baroque *ritardando* (rit.):

Practice Strategy

When you play a baroque piece, it should start and end relatively in the same tempo. It is musically correct, however, to make a slight *ritardando* at the end. This slowing down must not be overly done, or else it will not be characteristic of the time period. A good way to create a tasteful ending is to subdivide the beats. Allow the subdivisions to guide a natural and gradual lengthening of the beat. This will make the piece sound as though it is naturally coming to an end without too much extra time taken.

When you reach the last three measures of the piece, start to count and subdivide aloud, like this:

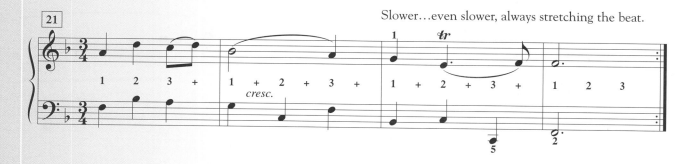

Listen to this practice strategy on the recording to further understand how much time to take.

Minuet in F major

George Frideric Handel
from *Suite in F major*, G. 179

(a) Optional trill:

N.B. Listen to the recording to hear how ornaments are added to decorate on the repeats.

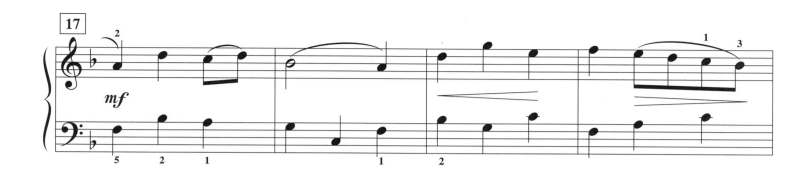

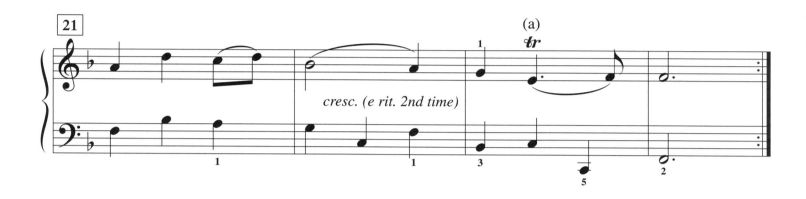

Sketch image of the first position in a minuet -
The Dancing Master by Pierre Rameau, 1731

ARIA

This piece is found in Handel's *Suite in D minor*.
An "Aria" is a song for voice and instrumental accompaniment.

Characteristics of the Baroque Era

Keyboard pieces were written without many articulations.

It is customary, when playing pieces by Handel, to group long sections of quarter notes into groups of two, as you see in the A section below. First play these measures without slurs, and then add them to hear the difference. This helps to make the piece sound more dance-like.

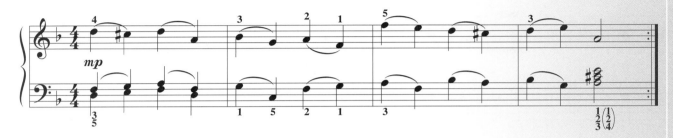

Listen to the recording to hear another way you can phrase the repeat of the A section.

Practice Strategy

Balancing the melody with the equally important bass line:

Look at the B section of the full score. Note that since the left hand is played *non legato*, the right hand can provide contrast if played *legato*. Balancing two voices in this way makes the piece much more interesting and allows both voices to be heard.

In order to hear the difference in articulation, experiment in the following three ways:

1) Play the left hand *legato* while playing the right hand *non legato*.

2) Next, play the right hand with the slurs marked in, and play the left hand completely *non legato* and detached.

3) Lastly, play the piece as it is marked. Listen for the phrase goals toward which the music naturally moves, and listen for the shorter notes as they slightly *crescendo* to a longer note. Hearing this on the recording will help you to understand this more easily.

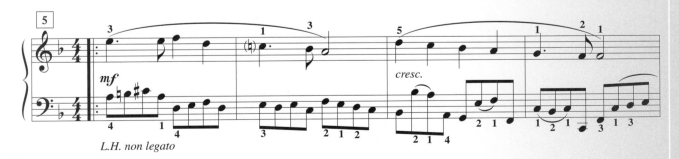

Which way does the B section sound better? When you are playing it correctly, you will provide contrast between the two hands, with the right-hand melody *legato* and the left-hand supportive accompaniment mostly *non legato*.

ARIA

George Frideric Handel
HWV 449

(b) Optional trill:

*Please see page eight for more information about this phrasing.

GAVOTTE IN G MAJOR

**Characteristics
of the
Baroque Era**

The gavotte originated as a folk dance from France and became a popular dance of the upper class from the late sixteenth century to the late eighteenth century. This particular piece is an example of a later type of gavotte, originating around the year 1660 and characterized by two quarter-note upbeats. The gavottes of this time had four-measure phrases.

This piece is from the *Aylesford Collection,* one of the largest and most comprehensive collections of Handel's music. This piece is simplified from the original to make it playable by student pianists.

**Practice
Strategy**

Slow vs. fast practicing (3 x 1 rule):
It is important to practice slowly as well as *a tempo* in order to be able to perform this piece well. Slow practice locks in the muscle memory and promotes accuracy and security, whereas *a tempo* practice encourages spontaneity, which is what happens in performance.

Using the 3 x 1 rule: Practice the following segments below by playing them three times slowly (no faster than ♪ = M.M. 144), and then one time, *a tempo* (♩ = M.M. 144). Listen for absolute evenness and clarity. Play the first eighth note without an accent and slightly *crescendo* to the longest note of the slur in order to give this gavotte its dance feel.

Segment #1

Beginning upbeats to the
downbeat of measure two:

Segment #2

Upbeats to measure three going
to the downbeat of measure four:

Segment #3

Upbeats to measure seven going
to the downbeat of measure eight:

Use this practice strategy
on all of the phrases!

GAVOTTE IN G MAJOR

George Frideric Handel
HWV 491

SARABANDE

**A sarabande is one of the four primary dances within a suite.
It is often the slowest dance and is usually in triple meter.**

**Characteristics
of the
Baroque Era**

In baroque music, small details are repeated continuously.

In this piece the ever-present two-note slurs change slightly. They are not duplicated exactly.

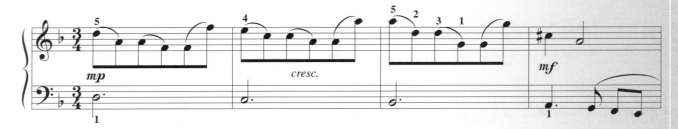

**Practice
Strategy**

Practicing two-note slurs:

Shaping the two-note slurs in this dance is essential. To do so, let your wrist drop and let your finger sink to the bottom of the key on the first note of each motive (denoted with a downward arrow.)

Drop your wrist here   Lift your wrist here

As you begin to play the last note of the two-note slur, lift your wrist and roll up on your fifth finger until you are playing on its fingertip, moving toward the fallboard of the piano (denoted with the upward arrow above).

The second note of the slur should sound lighter than the first note. Practice the drop and lift technique until you feel secure and comfortable.

Ask yourself after playing, "Did I produce a lovely, singing tone?"

"First beat" practice:

Practice Strategy

Here is another way to make your technique stay with you in performance:

1) Turn on your metronome to ♩ = M.M. 80.

2) Play the first downbeat of the piece and then lift your hands and follow the musical score with your eyes. Play the next downbeat, making sure to use the fingering that is marked in the score and that you stay in tempo with the metronome.

This practice strategy trains your eyes to look ahead and trains your ear to "hear" the music in your head as you prepare for each downbeat.

Picture of musicians performing, from *The Universal Musician*, 1731.

SARABANDE

George Frideric Handel
from *Suite in D Minor*, HWV 448

(a) Optional trill:

(a) The third beat of this measure can be played as two consecutive eighth notes for greater ease:

m. 7

m. 15 and m. 23

(c) Optional trill:

Within these sacred Walls the Memory of HANDEL was celebrated, under the patronage and in the presence of his most Gracious Majesty GEORGE the III. on the XXVI. and XXIX. of May, and on the III and V of June, MDCCLXXXIV. the Musick performed on this Solemnity, was selected from his own Works, under the direction of BROWNLOW Earl of Exeter, JOHN Earl of Sandwich, HENRY Earl of Uxbridge, Sir WATKIN WILL.m WYNN Bar.t and Sir RICHARD JEBB Bar.t the Band consisting of 525 Vocal & Instrumental Performers, was conducted by JOAH BATES Esq.r

GEORGE FREDERICK HANDEL Esq.r born February XXIII, MDCLXXXIV. died on Good Friday, April XIII, MDCCLIX.

E.F.Burney delin.

I.M.Delattre sculp.

J.F.Roubillac Sc.t

View of HANDEL'S Monument in Westminster Abbey.

Published January 14th 1785.

Sculpture of Handel at Westminster Abbey in London, England.

AIR IN B FLAT MAJOR

The use of the term "Air" began in France and England as far back as the sixteenth century. It was another word for "song," or "tune."

Creating clear passagework:

To articulate passages in baroque style, try the three following strategies:

1) Articulate each note well, always listening to each note's clarity.

2) Give each phrase a feeling of space and elegance.

3) Never push the tempo.

Practice Strategy

Creating the mood:

To communicate this piece to an audience, you may wish to think about the overall mood of the piece, so that you can bring the piece to life.

Listening to the recording, decide which of the following words best describe the piece. Create an image in your mind around the word you chose.

Practice Strategy

tense	*bold*	*graceful*
shocking	*jolly*	*persistent*
daring	*elegant*	*lilting*
tiny	*secure*	*refined*

AIR IN B FLAT MAJOR

George Frideric Handel
Aylesford Collection

(a) Optional trill:

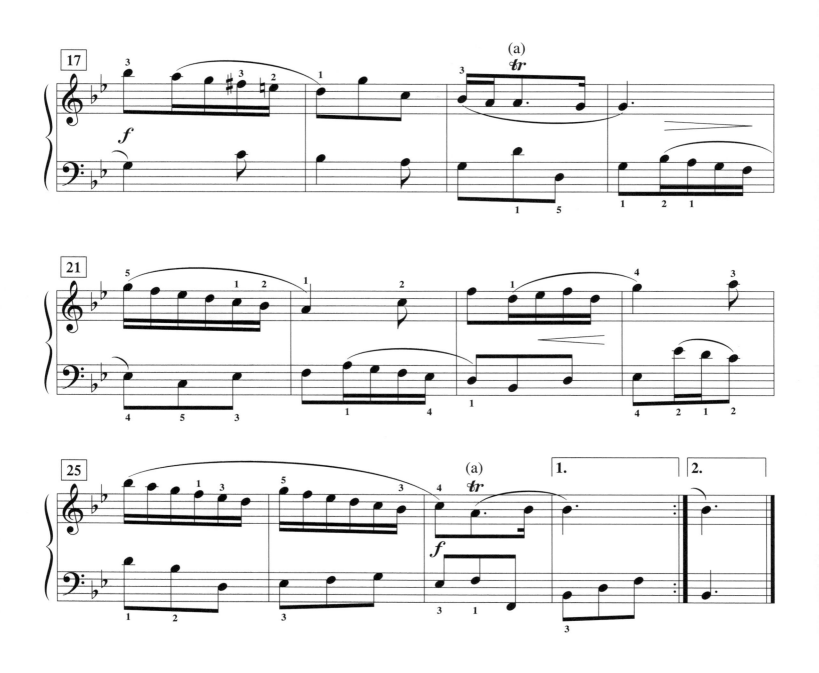

SONATINA IN G MAJOR

**Characteristics
of the
Baroque Era**

This piece displays an enduring energy.

From the very beginning of the piece, there is motion that does not stop until the final measure. This kind of activity is exciting to the ear because the forward motion is great. (See Bach's *Prelude in C major* as another example of this baroque characteristic.)

**Practice
Strategy**

"Smart" fingering:

One of the single most important things you can do to make your performance successful is to learn the correct fingering from the very first day of practice!

Here is the magical formula:

Divide the piece so that you are playing phrase fragments of seven notes or less, like this:

Measures 1-2, right hand:

Measures 1-2, left hand:

Measure 3, right hand:

Measures 3-4, left hand:

Play each fragment hands separately, *at least* five times in a row, correctly, before going on to the next fragment. If you make a mistake in fingering, notes, or rhythms, this does not count in the magical number of five. Follow this magical formula for every phrase in the entire sonatina.

SONATINA IN G MAJOR

George Frideric Handel
G. 234, HHA iv/6

*N.B. The longer slurs have been added to show the shape of the phrase.   (a) Optional trill:

DOMENICO SCARLATTI

(1685–1757)

Domenico Scarlatti, George Frideric Handel, and Johann Sebastian Bach were all born the same year, Bach and Handel in Germany, and Scarlatti in Naples, Italy. Domenico's famous father, Alessandro, was one of the most important composers of opera of his day. Alessandro taught his son how to sing, compose, and play the harpsichord and the organ.

When Domenico was sixteen, he became the organist and composer of the royal chapel in Naples, and began to compose operas himself. He also spent time in Venice and Rome with his father, always learning more and more about music.

When a harpsichord contest was held in Venice, Italy, Handel traveled there to compete, and met Scarlatti and his father. Though Handel was the better organist, both Handel and Scarlatti were outstanding keyboard players. The contest, which Scarlatti won, helped the two musicians to get to know one another, and they had a lasting friendship with mutual admiration.

At the age of twenty-four, Domenico became the music director for Queen Maria Casimira of Poland, who was living in Rome. After this post he went to Lisbon, Portugal, to become music director for the royal family, teaching music to the young Princess Maria Barbara and the other children in the royal court. His relationship with Maria Barbara lasted a lifetime. When she married and moved to Madrid in 1728, Scarlatti moved as well. When she became the queen of Spain, she made Scarlatti her court composer, and he spent the rest of his life in her palace.

Scarlatti was famous for his keyboard compositions and for his virtuosity at the instrument. He was over the age of fifty when he started to write his best works, his *Essercizi* for harpsichord. Among the *essercizi* (the Italian word for "exercises") were over 550 keyboard sonatas written for Maria Barbara! Most of these sonatas are in binary form. While Scarlatti's compositions express a full range of human emotion, he thought it was impolite to reveal any sadness. So his pieces are always light-hearted, or only slightly melancholy in tone. For the most part, they are joyful, spontaneous and melodious.

Alessandro Longo, from Naples, Italy, catalogued Scarlatti's works by key, which is why each piece has the abbreviation "L." Later, the influential harpsichordist by the name of Ralph Kirkpatrick catalogued Scarlatti's works again, which is why each piece has the abbreviation, "K."

MINUET IN G MINOR

Practice Strategy

Bringing a piece to life musically after it is learned:

In order to bring a piece to life for an audience, the tempo, the articulations, and the dynamics must be accurate. Listen to the recording of this piece, and think about the following musical ideas:

1) The tempo

Set your metronome at the following three tempos. Start at different places in the piece and concentrate on the steadiness of the beat throughout.

Which tempo feels the best to you?

2) The articulations

The different articulations between the hands make this piece interesting. Play the piece four times, each time paying careful attention to only *one* of the following points:

1) The lilt at the end of each three-note slur in the right hand. ❑

2) Every eighth note played in a detached, *non legato* style. ❑

3) Giving a little space between the quarter and eighth note figures in the left hand. ❑

4) The *legato* sound played only within the slurs. ❑

Check each box when you are sure you have focused on that particular point, and have played the entire piece with this in mind.

3) The dynamics

C.P. E. Bach, one of J.S. Bach's sons, wrote an *Essay on the True Art of Playing Keyboard Instruments*, which is still read by performers today. He wrote that it was important to play dynamics tastefully and that they should reflect the overall mood of the piece. Circle the one adjective which best illustrates this piece:

energetic   *lonely*   *cheerful*

perky   *harsh*   *sweet*

Minuet in G minor

Domenico Scarlatti
K. 88d/L. 36

(a) All eighth notes may be played *non legato*, unless marked otherwise.

*The roll is editorial.

Picture of a musician singing.
Notice the baroque clothing of the musician and the highly ornamented room
where he stands. From *The Universal Musician*, 1731.

MINUETTO IN C MAJOR

Characteristics of the Baroque Era

Characteristics of the era exemplified in this piece:

■ A melody created from short phrase fragments, as shown below:

Practice Strategy

The importance of "hands-alone" work:

To make sure that you are playing with consistent and detailed articulations, it is important that you spend part of your practice time every day playing through sections of this piece, hands apart, preferably with the metronome.

Practice Strategy

Creating perfect synchronization between the hands:

The repetitive phrases in this piece will be easier to play if you use the following steps when you practice:

1) On the second beat of every measure, lift your left hand and wrist. You will lift your left hand when you reach the last note of the three-note slur in the right hand, as shown below.

2) In perfect time, play the last note of the measure. Both of your hands will come off of the keys at the same time in order to prepare for the next downbeat.

MINUETTO IN C MAJOR

Domenico Scarlatti
K. 73b/L. 217

(a) Optional trill:

LARGHETTO IN D MINOR

Practice Strategy

How to add embellishments:

Once you can play this piece well *without* the ornaments, you can experiment with adding some. During the Baroque era, it was customary to add embellishments when repeating a section.

Some embellishments (ornaments) are easy to count with, while you may find it easier to play others by listening carefully to your teacher or to the recording and playing by ear.

Some ornaments are easier to play if you count the notes within the ornament so that they fall easily into place with the other hand.

For example, for measure eight, ornament (b), play and count several times, like this:

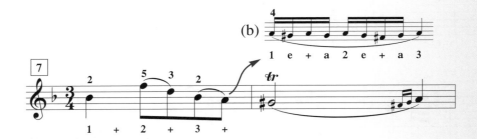

When you can do this comfortably, add the left-hand part, and play and count several times.

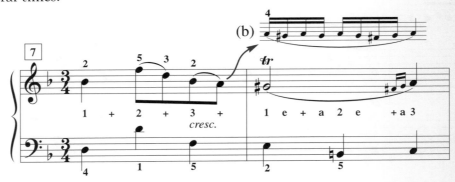

Embellishment (e) can also be easily counted. This way you will play the ornaments with great ease!

"Follow the leader."

Practice Strategy

Sometimes pianists get so focused on the right hand that they forget what is going on in the left hand. Let your left hand be the leader, and have your right hand follow it. Imagine that your left hand is the more important hand, and that the music of the left hand is what drives the rhythm and gives energy to the entire piece.

If you feel that your left hand is in complete control, this piece will be easy to play!

left hand **LEADS** *right hand follows*

LARGHETTO IN D MINOR

Domenico Scarlatti
K. 34/L. 7

(a) Optional trill (starting on downbeat):

(c) Optional trill:

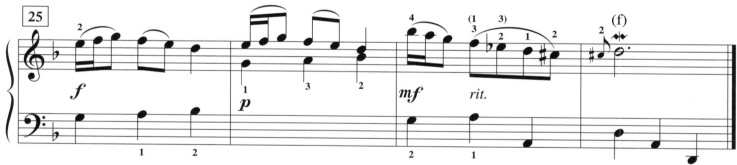

(d) Play these sixteenth notes on the beat.

(f)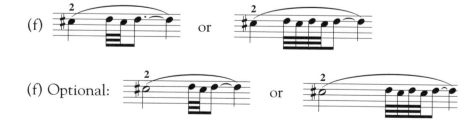

(f) Optional:

MINUETTO IN B FLAT MAJOR

Characteristics of the Baroque Era

Characteristics of the era to observe in this piece:

- Baroque music often uses one or two repetitive rhythms or patterns throughout a work. Which of the following rhythmic patterns do you see the most in your score? (Circle the correct one below.)

- This piece seems to be in a perpetual motion without any predictable cadences, except for those at the ends of both sections. Play the following melody in the right hand and notice that the only cadence, if any, is at the end of measure 16!

Practice Strategy

Balancing the melody with an equally important bass line:

Here is a practice plan that will work for you!

1) Practice hands separately and rhythmically, being sure to articulate each note correctly (slurred or detached). Listen carefully to hear space between notes that do not have slurs. Energize all leaps in the left hand.

2) Do not add any of the embellishments until you are completely comfortable with all of the notes and rhythms.

3) Then, hands together, practice very slowly (♪ = M.M. 104). This means that you will play one melodic note for every *two* ticks on your metronome! As shown below, play the first measure plus the downbeat of measure 2. Stop and repeat, like this:

Stop, then repeat several times.
Listen for clarity and evenness.

When you feel secure with the first measure, practice the second measure plus the downbeat of the third measure. Then practice measures three and four the same way. It is important to repeat each measure and the downbeat several times, always listening to yourself for balance, rhythm, and clarity.

Measure 2:

4) When comfortable, increase your tempo to ♩ = M.M. 104 and compare this to your slow practice. Is it just as clear and accurate?

5) Finally, practice all of these measures together as one continuous phrase.

REMEMBER, SLOW PRACTICE = QUICK RESULTS.

Playing with a *cantabile* sound:

The Italian term *cantabile* means to play in a "singing" manner. Always listen to yourself as you play, producing the most beautiful sound you can possibly achieve. The many turns in this piece ∽ are the perfect ornaments for making the melodic line attractive and brilliant. Each turn should completely and evenly fill a beat of music.

Practice Strategy

Minuetto in B flat major

Domenico Scarlatti
K. 42/L. 36

*The roll is editorial.

MINUETTO IN C MINOR

Minuetto, in Italian, is the same as the title word, "Minuet."

Characteristics of the Baroque Era

Characteristics of the era displayed in this piece:

■ Both sections ending with a trill.
■ Phrases not symmetrical.
■ Two melodic lines within the same hand, each called a "voice."

Notice the left hand in the B section:

This line of music is called the "tenor" voice (the note stems go up)...

...while this line of music is called a "bass" voice (the note stems go down).

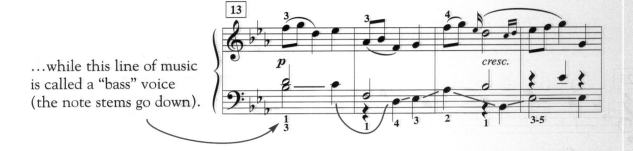

Practice Strategy

How to practice different voices within the same hand:

In the same practice session, practice the left hand in the following ways:

1) Play only the tenor voice, with the correct fingering, as outlined above.

2) Then, play only the bass voice, with the correct fingering. You will notice that some of the notes are both tenor and bass voices, since the stems go *both* ways!

3) Now play both voices together, thinking about them as two different instruments playing at the same time.

Below is a copy of Domenico Scarlatti's *Minuetto*. This is called a facsimile, because it is an exact copy of his manuscript. Look at the differences between the copy and the same piece in modern notation on pages 80 and 81. Observe the absence of fingering, articulations, and dynamics. Notice that the first eight measures are written in the treble clef and the tenor clef. The tenor clef indicates the position of middle C, which is the second line down on the staff.

Characteristics of the Baroque Era

Facsimile of *Minuetto in C minor - K. 40*

FJH1438

MINUETTO IN C MINOR

Domenico Scarlatti
K. 40/L. 357

(b) The sixteenth note is played on the downbeat.

VOLUME ONE – REPERTOIRE WITH THEIR SOURCES

Sources consulted for this edition:

Bach, Johann Sebastian. Die Klavierbüchlein für Anna Magdalena Bach (1722), (1725).
    Edited by Georg Von Dadelsen. Bärenreiter, Kassel: Basel: London.

Bach, Johann Sebastian. Neue Bach Ausgabe (NBA).

Bach, Johann Sebastian. Works from the Wilhelm Friedemann Bach Notebook.

Bach, Johann Sebastian. Clavierwerke, Breitkopf & Härtel, Leipzig.

Handel, George Frideric. Hallische Händel-Ausgabe (HHA).

Handel, George Frideric. The Works of George Frideric Handel, ed. Friedrich Chrysander.
    Neue Ausgabe Sämtlicher Werke (NBA).

Handel, George Frideric. Zwanzig Klavierstücke, ed. Willy Rehberg. B. Schott's Söhne, Mainz und Leipzig.

Handel, George Frideric. Klavierwerke IV, ed. Terence Best. Bärenreiter, Kassel: Basel: Tours: London.

Scarlatti, Domenico. Complete Keyboard Works – in facsimile from the manuscript and printed sources.
    Edited by Ralph Kirkpatrick. Johnson Reprint Corporation, NY and London: 1972.

GLOSSARY OF MUSICAL TERMS
Tempo markings

Allegro	*Allegretto*	*Moderato*	*Andante*	*Grave*
cheerful, bright, faster than *allegretto*	same feeling as *allegro*, but not as fast	a moderate tempo	walking tempo	slow, solemn

Accompaniment – a musical background for a principal part. The background may be the left hand of a keyboard composition or orchestral background for a solo instrument. The accompaniment provides harmony for the melody.

Articulation – the manner of playing; the touch. Refers to how notes are attacked, sustained, or accented — *legato, staccato,* etc.

a tempo – return to the regular tempo, especially after a *ritardando*.

Binary form – a piece built in two parts (AB); the first part sometimes ends on the tonic but most of the time ends on the dominant chord (V), and the second part ends on the tonic. Both parts are usually marked to be repeated before going on.

Bourée – a dance that originated in France. It was fast, in duple meter, and was popular during the 17th and 18th centuries.

Cantabile – an Italian term for "singing."

Countermelody – a musical line different from that of the primary melody. A countermelody can be part of an accompaniment.

Counterpoint – two melodies played simultaneously as different voices.

Downbeat – the first beat of a full measure, or the downward motion of a conductor's hand.

Embellishment – also called ornamentation. The way composers fill out or decorate the texture, making the sound more grand.

Figured bass – numbers marked in the bass line that designated the harmonies from which an accompaniment was improvised by the performer.

Gavotte – This dance originated as a folk dance in France, becoming a popular dance of the court from the late sixteenth century to the late eighteenth century.

Homophonic texture – a melody supported by harmonies. The melodic voice is often in the right hand with chords in the left, to create the harmony. It can also be done the other way around, melody in the left hand and chords above.

Imitation – when a melodic idea is heard in one voice and then heard in another voice.

Improvisation – music that is created at the exact same time it is being performed.

Minuet – an elegant dance in triple meter, first introduced during the time of Louis XIV around the year 1650. It became a movement in the baroque suite.

Motive – a short melodic or rhythmic pattern (a few pitches) from which a full melodic and rhythmic phrase may grow.

(N.B.) *Nota Bene* – a Latin phrase meaning, "mark well." Used to point out something important.

Ostinato – one of the voices in a piece, such as the bass line, that repeats over and over again.

Phrase goal – the place toward which the music naturally moves, just as, when we speak, our sentences move toward a word with slightly more emphasis or volume than others. Let your ear be your guide and follow this rise of melody toward a goal. After arrival at its goal, the phrase naturally tapers.

Polyphonic texture – music with several lines (two or more) instead of a single melody and an accompaniment.

Rounded binary form – a piece in regular binary form, with one difference: the opening tune of the A section returns within the B section to lead back to a nice ("rounded") conclusion for the piece.

Suite – A collection of dance-inspired movements that are in the same key, but are different in tempo, meter, and character. "Suite" is synonymous with the title word, "Partita."

Ternary form – music that has three sections, ABA or ABC.

Trill – an ornament consisting of a repetitive alternation of a note with the note a whole step or half step above it. The ornament usually begins above the principal note in the Baroque and Classical eras.

Upbeat – one or more notes in an incomplete measure occurring before the first bar line of a piece or section of music; sometimes called a *pickup*.